TITIAN

The life and work of the artist illustrated with 80 colour plates

ALESSANDRO BALLARIN

THAMES AND HUDSON

Translated from the Italian by Pearl Sanders

Printed in Italy

Life and Works

> Direct contact with the substance which they [Michelangelo and Titian] handled all their lives seems to have been the mystical source of a superhuman vigour.
>
> H. Tietze

It is certain that Titian grew up in an atmosphere of violent controversy, so that historians find it impossible to construct an ordered pattern of affiliations between master and pupil, of heritages handed down and quietly perpetuated. We know from sixteenth-century historians all about the polemics out of which young artists often emerged – about pupils whose success exceeded that of their teacher, and the disappointment of the teacher when the pupil took all credit upon himself. The origins of Titian are to be found in that still unresolved mystery, the personality of Giorgione, and especially in the decoration of the Fondaco dei Tedeschi. It is known that Giorgione painted frescoes on the main façade overlooking the Grand Canal, while Titian, in a subordinate capacity, decorated the sides of the building which faced the streets. The year was 1508, when, according to modern calculations, Titian must have been about twenty. Giorgione was to die prematurely two years later in the plague of 1510. Sebastiano del Piombo, Giorgione's other great pupil, was a little more than twenty, while Bellini, who in 1506 was still considered by Dürer to be the most robust of Venetian painters and still effectively held his own against younger generations of artists, was almost an octogenarian.
The frescoes for the Fondaco dei Tedeschi would seem to mark the first appearance in Venice of the spatial concepts familiar to Tuscan art, where space was built up by rhythm and depended on a new relationship between the figures and the architectonic background. These new ideas were far more likely to find a fertile soil in the two younger artists, Titian and Sebastiano del Piombo, who were eager to absorb new experiences, than in Giorgione whose personality,

as we know from paintings prior to this date, was already formed (*The Storm*, Venice, Accademia). Some faint signs of this new trend had already appeared in the altarpiece painted by Bellini in 1506 for the church of San Zaccaria, but it was probably due to the fact that Fra Bartolommeo was present in Venice in 1508 that these ideas were propagated. Giorgione was the first to adopt them and he carried with him his two pupils: Sebastiano, who followed the precepts of classicism rather literally, and Titian, whose interpretation of classicism was more personal as it was transposed into the terms of Venetian art.

To judge from the few remaining fragments and from the engravings made by Zanetti in the eighteenth century of the already much-damaged frescoes, Titian was moving away from Giorgione in his conception of space, which was closer to that of Renaissance artists. Since these frescoes are lost, and space does not permit a consideration of how the gap in the study of Titian's early career can be partly filled by the large group of works in which art historians have come to recognize Titian's hand, we must pass to 1511, the date of the frescoes in the Scuola del Santo, Padua, and other works of the same period.

In two portraits (*pl. 7* and *p. 5*) in the National Gallery, London, the colour intensity is enhanced by the vitality of the figures, by their powerful physical presence, the way they look out over an elongated perspective beyond the plane of a window-sill, or are placed at the side of the composition in a manner intended to provide the widest possible surface for colour and to resolve the three-dimensional reality of the figure in the broad expanse of colour. The distinguishing feature of Titian's painting, especially when compared with that of his imitators, lies in these expanses of colour. They are always a means of visualizing the movement of a figure and surprising it in that split second, non-existent in the temporal continuity of actual experience, when it reveals itself most completely. At this point, movement has slowed to a halt, and it becomes possible to enjoy the sight of an upright cuff in the sleeve of a dress, or a shirt open just enough to show a patch of healthy naked flesh, or a neck emerging from the folds of a fur collar. But it is clear that

Portrait of a Man (*see p. 40*).

this is an instant of repose within a movement, since the planes, including those produced by the figures portrayed, are always curved, in tension, so as to generate the space of the composition. For example, in the *Portrait of a Man* in the National Gallery, London (*above*), the sitter is shown through the unfolding of a few broad planes of colour. The curved planes making up the figure are not present in a pre-existent space, but themselves generate the space of the painting, through a calm yet energetic movement of outlines and luminous surfaces. Space is therefore architecturally constructed, and exemplified in an archetype of humanity, as was always the case in Renaissance painting. Titian is unique in that space is captured in the process of its creation.

In addition to what he learned from Giorgione, Titian inherited from the tradition of the Italian fifteenth century, from Piero della Francesca to Bellini, that capacity for perceiving reality in the guise of space filled with colour applied in zones and given perspective by means of light. At the same time, he understood wherein the originality of Giorgione lay: in enriching the tonal qualities of colour and so making it possible to construct space through a tonal orchestration instead of through a synthesis of perspective in the fifteenth-century manner, and thus being able to represent distance and atmosphere as well as the living quality of the flesh. The advent of Titian therefore marks a vigorous return to the naturalistic tradition of Piero and Bellini, on which from the earliest stages in his career Giorgione had turned his back in order to experiment with the possibilities of a 'modern manner... without [outline] drawing' (Vasari), although in this respect Titian soon showed himself to be a faithful follower of Giorgione. From the very first a strong naturalistic tendency made its appearance in the work of Titian, independently of the painting of the recent past, which still lived in the mastery of Bellini, and of the painting of the present, growing unpredictably in the hands of Giorgione. It was soon obvious that Giorgione's brand of naturalism would not have led to the naturalism of modern art, but to a final rebirth of the Greece of Phidias. However, what came out of this naturalism did in fact show modern tendencies and entered the tradition of modern art from other directions, in the highly complicated framework of influences and affiliations which makes up its origins. An outstanding example is Titian's *Portrait of a Girl* in Vienna (*pl. 17*), which attains the immediacy and freshness of a Manet. It is one of the most amazing works of Titian's early period. The simplicity of the colour planes, the black cloak sliding off the girl's shoulder and held back by her hand, the low-cut dress, the youthful complexion and shining mass of fair hair, reveal the rapidly visualized, living presence of the young girl. When we think of Bellini's last portraits, still held in the tight formal perspective of the fifteenth century, or even of the timidly portrayed figures of Giorgione, we see immediately the revolution Titian

brought to painting in the revelation of naked female flesh, of fair hair lying loose on the shoulders, of black cloak and white blouse, realized as if by instinct under the urgency of Titian's compulsion to naturalism.
In the three works in the Scuola del Santo, Padua, the planes making up the figures and those making up the architectonic background are joined by a feeling of monumentality and action new to the tradition of Bellini and Giorgione (*pl. 6*). In *St Anthony Healing a Newborn Child*, Titian divides up the space between the side containing the building, where the marble of a classical statue vibrates with life, and the landscape; in the foreground broad zones of colour are linked through a powerful interplay of curves, creating a rhythmic equilibrium which has caused this painting to be justly compared with Raphael's *Mass of Bolsena*, in the Vatican, as an example of a complete realization of Renaissance ideas occurring in the early years of the century. Titian held firmly to this classical manner up to the time of the Frari *Assumption* (1518). The starting-point of this phase lay in the intuition he had at the time of the Fondaco frescoes that a modern style of painting must necessarily depend on broad sweeping rhythms so as to set the figure in high relief, in a new relationship with the architectonic section of the composition, and causing the illuminated expanses of colour to coincide with the rhythmically curving planes. The development and interplay of fields of colour was conditioned by the development of these curving planes. In the Uffizi *Flora*, the expansive sweeps of colour under the action of light become united with the majestic movement of the curve which outlines the figure, leaning forward slightly to offer flowers. When we compare this with a similar figure painted by Palma Vecchio, we realize to what extent Titian's colour-plane generates the space of the painting. Titian's figures always form a spatial entity, an architecture of space set down in the process of its construction.
In his portraits Titian constructs 'grandiose existences' (Burckhardt, *Cicerone*, 1855), spatial entities removed from the wear of time and the temporal dimensions of our worldly experience, yet endowed with the vitality of living creatures. The *Portrait of a Man* in Vienna (*pl. 27*), at one

time wrongly identified as a portrait of the physician Parma, is an example of the way in which the reality of a portrait is removed from the corrosive action of time, and is seen rather as the result of a process of growth starting in the shapeless wall of the background and culminating in the construction of a person. The space is generated by a process through which the image grows out of the background, which is shadowy and atmospheric, as if the figure had assumed so imposing a physical presence that it became set apart from the depredations of time. The scarcely thinning white hair, the bull-neck, left bare by the open shirt and coat, the protruding lower lip, the hooked nose in relief against the flat forehead, and the penetrating gaze emphasize the powerful atmosphere.

Although Titian's method of creating space in the architecture of a human figure still occurs here within the Renaissance framework of an enclosed space and reaffirms the Renaissance conception of man as the centre of the universe, it introduces a new element of vitality and, one might say, of time, which led to the idea of existential man and became a model to later painters. However, Titian's creation of space is very different from the same phenomenon in the works of Caravaggio or Velázquez, where the essential condition is the degradation of the human figure to an object of the painter's analysis, subjected to a process of corruption and enfeebling. With Titian the growth of space is a powerful affirmation of a reality pulsating with life, but invested with a timelessness and an uncontaminated beauty which make it a classical art.

In his *Assumption* Titian provides a significant indication of a new dramatic direction by depicting the event in its final stage, with the Madonna rising to heaven on a cloud among a band of exultant angels and apostles in various attitudes. But it is light which is really the dramatic element in this composition, a yellow glow which bursts forth from the heavenly regions and descends through the wind-tossed clouds, creating areas of light and shade among the group of apostles. The idea of introducing movement into the composition of this group by the expedient of cloud reveals Titian's naturalistic and dramatic temperament.

The vast size of the work, and the distance from which it had to be viewed at the far end of the spacious Gothic nave, excited Titian's feeling for construction and naturalism, and led him to treat the subject very freely, with broad brushstrokes, daring touches of light, and flowing lines to mark the shadow. Those places where the forms are blurred because of their proximity to the powerful source of light, as in the *putti* nearest to God the Father, are counter-balanced by the bold naturalistic treatment of the apostles. The areas of shadow throw into relief the luminous red robe of the apostle on the left and the white sleeve of the older man beside him. This powerful naturalism becomes one and the same thing as the movement implicit in the fall of light. The *Assumption* marks a decisive stage in the course of Titian's art, and its importance was immediately confirmed by the three works painted for Alfonso d'Este in Ferrara, *Worship of Venus* (Madrid, Prado), *Bacchanal* (*pl. 28-9*) and *Bacchus and Ariadne* (London, National Gallery), all executed between 1518 and 1523.
After his series of paintings on dramatic themes executed at the time of the Scuola del Santo works, Titian had turned for preference to the subjects of 'female half-figures' and groups of three figures in 'Seductions', 'Concerts' and 'Sacred Conversations'. The paintings executed for Alfonso d'Este represented something new, following the line of the *Assumption*. With these three works we see clearly that the period inaugurated by the Frari *Assumption* was characterized by a striving after a more intensely dramatic function of space, and the result of Titian's research at this period was a manner we might call 'pre-baroque'. It was no mere chance that led Rubens and Poussin to copy the *Bacchanal*. We need only compare *Sacred and Profane Love* (*pl. 24-5*) with the *Bacchanal*, which is separated from it by only about four years. In the *Bacchanal*, the contrast between two masses – the dense mass of trees and the mass of luminous clouds – introduces a contrast of light and shade which determines the placing of the bacchantes in the composition, and the bright light falling on the slope where Silenus lies on his back emphasizes the naturalistic element. In the serene composition of *Sacred and Profane Love*, a

small number of broad colour surfaces produce a simplicity which is classical in being translated into pure rhythm, into the substance of space and the architecture of colour. In the *Bacchanal*, Titian's naturalism is closer to the early baroque in manner, and has moved away from classicism. This is seen in the prominence given to the young bacchante dressed in white among the three figures in half-shadow, and in the prominence of the naked body of Ariadne reclining in the foreground, in the full glare of light. In *Sacred and Profane Love*, where space is generated and measured by the curving planes of the figures, and focused by the rhythm which unites the figures on the edge of the composition in an arch formation and appears confined by the architectonic form, there is a restlessness and agitation which reflect a first awareness of what was then taking place in the art of central Italy. The figure construction takes into account both its sculptural aspect and inherent movement, following the example of the painting of central Italy, while nature, animated by a new sense of light, is represented with greater freedom and breadth.
At about the same period in Titian's career, he achieved similar effects in the altarpiece in Ancona (1520), and in the polyptych in Brescia (1520-2), of which the *Resurrection of Christ* forms the central panel. Here the effect is of a night scene torn apart by the first light of dawn – 'in the sky the clouds are chased by gusts of wind which stir the shroud and banner of Christ and almost tear them off' (Cavalcaselle). The figure of Christ rises in a position recalling the *Laocoön*, of which it is known that Titian possessed a copy. Later, in the third decade of the century, the *Entombment*, in the Louvre (*pl. 34-5*), again reveals the new direction Titian was taking when we compare it with paintings of the middle years of the second decade, such as the *Virgin and Child with saints and donor*, formerly in the Doria Balbi collection and now in a private collection at Reggio Emilia. In the latter painting the curved planes formed by the figures of the Virgin and St Catherine on one side and of St Dominic and the donor on the other generate the space of the painting and at the same time close it in, in the sense that the space comes to be resolved in a pulsating

architecture of colour masses, arched 'according to the dramatic principle of the meeting point' (Pallucchini). The surfaces are broken up by contrasting areas of light and shade (the shapes forming the black clothes of the donor and St Dominic stand out against the brightly-lit landscape, while the luminous dress of the Virgin is set against the dark part of the wall) so as to achieve the classical treatment of colour to which Titian was aspiring at that time. In this arrangement we can again perceive the heritage of the spatial-perspective concepts of the best fifteenth-century tradition.

In the *Entombment*, the figures are made to bend over the body of Christ, not for an architectonic purpose or in order to enclose the space of the painting, but to express emotion, and the composition of the figures is the more effective for the contrast between luminous areas and areas under shadow. The heightened emotion is echoed in the sunset sky rent by clouds, and the dramatic effect is increased by its horizontal line. Here the sky is not depicted as a plane of luminous colour, but moves freely and forms the space Titian now needed in order to give free rein to his emotion. The sunset is not represented objectively, as in the work of modern artists, but as a projection of Titian's sensibility. Then there is the amazing treatment of the two female figures, who seem so much a part of the sky – an effect achieved by means of the luminous quality of the blue cloak worn by Mary, which is not so brilliant a blue as we find in details of paintings done ten years earlier, but glows with the warm light of sunset. The *Entombment* concludes the period of experimentation begun by the *Bacchanal* and the Brescia polyptych, but has these additional emotional overtones.

The altarpiece painted for the Pesaro family and placed on one of the side altars of Santa Maria de' Frari in 1526 would seem to close the period in Titian's art which had begun with the *Assumption* in the same church and was characterized by a pre-baroque naturalism. At the same time it marks the beginning of another phase during which he dwelt more and more on monumental architectonic themes of a direct classical origin. An innovation was brought into the composition of the altarpiece by placing the steps and two tall columns at an oblique angle, and by the very daring device of placing the Virgin at the apex of a pyramid, the base of which is formed by the members of the Pesaro family, while the patron saints Peter and Anthony are placed in the intermediate position. A banner with the coats of arms of the Pesaro and Borgia families counter-balances the angle of the Virgin's head and at the same time serves to underline the prestige of the Pesaro family, especially Jacopo Pesaro, who stands alone on the left of the composition. A cloud on which angels stand bearing the Cross passes in front of the columns and casts a shadow over them. This shadow creates an illusionistic effect, causing the planes to stand apart from each other and the columns to recede towards the sky which forms the background to the scene. In spite of the absolute originality of this invention, however, the work is not convincing on the poetic plane, and the cloud which passes across the foreground, casting a shadow, remains only an illusionistic banality. The real qualities of this painting lie in its details and in the portraits, especially those of the marginal and younger figures. The representation of the older ones is too highly individualized in the recognizable features of each character and in a too obvious mimicry, where a contributing factor is without doubt the profile view, as though Titian had painted them in the spirit of Gentile Bellini. The desire to praise the Pesaro family detracts from the quality of the painting, and although that is not too serious in this case, it does point to a problem which was to be with Titian until at least 1540. The illusionistic expedient of the cloud and the too illustrative treatment of the portraits are the visible signs of the crisis of classical naturalism through which Titian was passing at this time and of his ability to recognize and represent reality in the form in which it was expressed in the High Renaissance style of his youth. The unified vision which had nourished Titian's early years up to the time of the *Assumption* had become less evident in the years between the *Assumption* and the last of the three *Bacchanals* painted for Alfonso d'Este. It was a vision in which every classical impulse became resolved into a spectacle of nature and life, and nature was transposed into an architecture of space. However, it could not withstand the pressure of new experiences, arising out of Titian's encounter with new artistic circles.

The problem, and the terms in which it was made apparent, cannot be understood apart from a consideration of the circles in which Titian moved during the third and fourth decades of the century: the courts of Federigo Gonzaga in Mantua and Francesco Maria della Rovere in Urbino. During his early years Titian had obtained commissions almost exclusively from local Venetian families, the same who had supported Giorgione. But now commissions came from farther afield and eventually included the greatest figures in European politics. The years before and after 1520 were marked by Titian's relations with the Este Court of Alfonso I, Duke of Ferrara, and the series of *Bacchanals* painted for the Duke's study can be better understood against the background of the Este circle. Here the culture of the Renaissance was substantially maintained but with the infiltration of certain esoteric elements, fully expressed later in the art of Dosso. An entirely different context was provided for the works executed for the Dukes of Mantua and Urbino in the 1530s. The work relationship with the Duke of Mantua, although dating from 1523, did not become fully operative until after Titian's visit to Mantua in 1527-8, and was especially important in the fourth decade of the century, culminating in the commission for the *Twelve Caesars* to be painted for the Ducal Palace in Mantua. From 1524, Giulio Romano, one of Raphael's most important pupils, worked in the court of the Gonzaga as a supervisor of the workshops of the Tea Palace and the new apartments of the Ducal Palace. It was for one of the rooms in these new apartments that Titian executed the *Twelve Caesars*. In the 1520s and '30s Mantua became a fortress of Roman culture, and the mannerism introduced through this culture had decisive consequences for Venetian art. Titian's relations with the Duke of Urbino occurred between 1532 and 1539; a large series of commissions resulted, and these fully occupied Titian during those years. He did not have occasion to go to Urbino before 1545, yet he must have been aware of the works which, from about 1530 onwards, a group of artists had been producing on the orders of the Duchess Eleonora Gonzaga in the old fifteenth-century surroundings of the Imperial Villa above Pesaro. These artists included followers of Raphael, among them Luca Penni and Raffaellino del Colle, and others like the Dossi brothers, working under the direction of Genga on the construction of a new villa in the style of the Roman Renaissance by the side of the old one. Titian must therefore have been familiar with the cultural atmosphere of the court and with the requirements of the Duke as patron. From 1527 Pietro Aretino was in Venice, and Titian had formed a close friendship with him. Aretino played no small part in introducing the name of his friend to the foreign courts. Thanks to the social contacts he made in this way, Titian twice met the Emperor Charles V, between 1529 and 1533, on the two occasions when he visited Bologna. On the second visit he received from the Emperor the title of Palatine Count, an honour which included the title of ' Nobles of the Empire ' for his children and ' Knight of the Golden Spur ' for himself; this gave him free access to the court.

To return to the paintings, in the *Portrait of Federigo Gonzaga* in the Prado, painted in the second half of the 1520s, a new element had already appeared which was absent from the portraits of the first part of the decade, like the *Portrait of a Man*, sometimes known as *Man with a Glove* (*pl. 33*). Unfortunately, we have lost the work which would have thrown the greatest light on the new problems faced by Titian during the fourth decade of the century: the *Death of St Peter the Martyr*, painted in the years 1528-30 for the Venetian church of SS. Giovanni e Paolo. Vasari's enthusiasm is in itself a significant indication of the new development in Titian's work, and we can also gain some insight into the form it took from engravings made after the lost painting, in which we see that the influence of Raphael was paramount. Titian must have prepared this work for the competition organized by the Confraternity of San Pietro Martire in 1528, not long after the visit or visits he made to Mantua in 1527-8. There he could have seen what

was being done following on from Raphael's last years, and it is by no means impossible that on his return to Venice to take part in the competition – in which his most dangerous rival was not Palma Vecchio, but Pordenone – he was influenced by *The Conversion of St Paul*, one of the series of cartoons executed by Raphael for the Sistine Chapel tapestries. This was one of Raphael's last works, and was in the collection of the Grimani family in Venice. With the loss of such important works as *Votive Banner of the Doge Andrea Gritti*, painted for the Ducal Palace of Venice (1531), *Annunciation*, for the church of Santa Maria degli Angeli, Murano (1537), *Twelve Caesars*, for Mantua (1537-8), and the great *Battle of Cadore*, for the Great Counsel Chamber of the Ducal Palace (1537-8), it becomes difficult to piece together the history of this decade. We know that Titian's art fluctuated between a manneristic and an archaic style, and that this alternation has sometimes led art historians to date the paintings wrongly, as in the case of the *St Nicholas* altarpiece for the Frari Church, now in the Vatican Museum, the *Assumption* in Verona Cathedral, and the fragmentary fresco of a *Madonna and Child* in the Ducal Palace. Reference has been made to the group of works painted for the Court of Urbino, now in the Pitti and Uffizi (*pl.37*).
The Magdalen (*pl. 36*) is a study of a nude painted with robust naturalism and with an illusionistic quality (see the effect of the bright tawny hair). Faced with this 'unspontaneous naturalistic illusionism' (Pallucchini), one longs for a return to the manner of treating the nude in Titian's early *Sacred and Profane Love* (*pl. 24-5*). *The Magdalen* is an excellent illustration of Titian's frequent recourse during this period to a classical reference, in order to create a new image (an antique statue of Venus is thought to have been the model for this painting). At the same time, the work is executed in a vein of illustration which borders on illusionism, thus breaking up the unified vision exemplified in *Sacred and Profane Love*. The *Portrait of Francesco Maria della Rovere* provides another example of illusionistic banality: the arm clothed in armour and carrying the staff of office appears to emerge out of the framework of the composition, and the planes recede deeper and deeper into the

background. In this case also there is a rhetorical classicism together with an illustrativeness of detail, to emphasize the prestige of the Duke, the helmet and insignia forming a harmonious arrangement behind his head. Titian was, of course, too great an artist to remain long diverted from his chosen course, and even if we seek only among the works of this period which have survived, there is no lack of a high poetic content, where landscape forms the most significant element and there are no architectonic details: *The Madonna with Child, St John and St Catherine*, in the National Gallery, London, the *Madonna of the Rabbit* and the so-called *Pardo Venus* (*pl. 38-9*), beside which one might place the masterpiece of the Urbino series, the famous *Venus of Urbino* (Uffizi).

In the *Pardo Venus*, against an expansive background of exuberant nature, filled with woods, streams and river banks, and inhabited by satyrs and nymphs, Zeus transformed into a satyr surprises Antiope asleep, and uncovers her nakedness. A youth leaves for the hunt to the sound of horns, while in the distance, on the banks of a stream, the hunt is already in full swing and the dogs have scented a stag. These episodes, which are not linked by narrative, have their purpose and the reason for their existence in the vitality of nature. The excitement of the youth as he sets off for the hunt, like the insidious gesture of Zeus as he uncovers the nakedness of Antiope, find in a nature vibrant with life the complicity needed for this ravishment of the senses. Although there are archaic elements in this work and a certain rigidity in the composition, due probably to the fact that it was painted over a long period of time, it has a special importance because it is here that we see the beginning of Titian's interest in mythological themes, as it was to reappear many times in later years in the paintings of *Venus with the Organ-player* (*pl. 46-7*) and the *poesie* for Philip II. The gesture of Zeus uncovering the nymph is a forerunner to the theme of the organ-player turning to look at Venus as she lies naked on the bed, while the youth setting off with dogs for the hunt foreshadows Adonis freeing himself from the embrace of Venus in the Prado *Venus and Adonis*.

A new stage was reached in the history of Titian's relations with mannerism in the years around 1540, within the framework of a situation which was to have a considerable effect on Venetian art. The period of Palma Vecchio, Cariani, Sebastiano del Piombo, Bonifazio Veronese, which arose in Titian's early years, finally declined. Pordenone, who had kept the tradition of Roman culture alive in Venice, died in 1539. Lotto, the only artist of sufficient stature to be considered in the same terms as Titian, had retired to spend the last years of his lonely existence in the monastery of Loreto, where he died in 1556. His career, like that of Savoldo, a Brescian living in Venice, forms part of the history of the first half of the century, providing a type of painting which was virtually an alternative to Titian's classicism. However, because Titian always looked outward to the mannerism of central Italy, these artists came to seem confined within a narrow provincialism. New names, of painters who were twenty years of age or a little older about the year 1540, then came to the fore in Venetian painting: Andrea Schiavone, Jacopo Bassano and Jacopo Tintoretto. Titian, whose life spanned most of the sixteenth century, formed a bridge between the two periods. The younger generation recognized signs of a new direction in his painting from the time of the *Death of St Peter the Martyr*, but were more eager to adopt the forms of mannerism, as it reached Venice in 1540. Titian was not prepared to do the same, and this led to a break which was not mended until he was a very old man. In the period of years which saw the arrival in Venice of Francesco Salviati with his pupil Giuseppe Porta (1539) and of Vasari (1541), Titian must have been the first to show a keen interest in the 'manner' of these Tuscan artists. The influence of Salviati is apparent in a number of works painted between 1540 and 1544: *The Address of Alfonso d'Avalos*, 1540-1 (*pl. 41-2*), *Portrait of Ranuccio Farnese* (Washington, National Gallery, Kress Collection, 1542), *The Crown of Thorns*, *c.* 1542 (*pl. 43*), *Ecce Homo* (Vienna, Kunsthistorisches Museum, 1543), *St John the Baptist* (Venice, Accademia), *The Vision of St John the Evangelist* (Washington, National Gallery, Kress Collection, *c.* 1544) and the

three ceilings for Santo Spirito (Venice, Salute Church, 1542-4).
In the landscapes Titian painted in the fourth and fifth decades of the century there is a noticeable influence of the art of Salviati, combined with that of Raphael and the school of Mantua. This would be seen more clearly, if we could reconstruct the lost *Twelve Caesars* and *Battle of Cadore*, as a more turgid and declamatory manner but with less ornamentation. The example of ' style ' inherent in the ' manner ' of Salviati proved, I believe, a decisive factor in the solution of the crisis in Titian's painting, in liberating it from certain ambiguities present in the preceding period. The accent shifted from an insistence on naturalism so great as to lead to the extreme of illusionistic effect found in the works of that period, and moved to a rigid formal treatment which restricted the space in the composition to the foreground, by means of a series of ' figures ' typical of the manneristic repertory. Forms were decomposed and formed again in a more dignified pattern. In a ' figure ' which much preoccupied Titian during these years, the limbs turned into a scorpion's tentacles radiating from the body, which thinned out into a single leg: this appears in the Salute ceilings. Another typical ' figure ' had bent arms forming a pattern of broken lines in the shape of a letter Z in relation to the axis of the body, placed in relief by the lance of a halberd: we find this in the soldiers in *The Address of Alfonso d'Avalos* and *Ecce Homo*. In these cases, which are not unique, the impression given is that the figure is embossed by a seal – an idea of form and beauty which was certainly manneristic in origin and foreign to the creative processes of Titian during his youth and during the 1530s. The formal tension implicit in the ' manner ' of Salviati had destroyed all Titian's naturalistic tendencies and even the classical inclination of works executed for the courts of Mantua and Urbino. The particular form of mannerism taken by Salviati led Titian to adopt a restricted and dynamic view of space and to exclude a broad narrative treatment. The Prado *Address of Alfonso d'Avalos* (*pl. 41-2*) is a turning-point in Titian's art. I do not think I am reading too much into the passage of the letter Aretino

wrote to Avalos in 1540, when he went into a long eulogy of the painting which was still in progress. He showed a keen awareness of the formal innovations of the painting – so keen, in fact, that it might be supposed he was recording Titian's own impression, or at any rate remembering the discussions he had enjoyed with his friend, possibly as they wandered through the Ca' Grimani, where Francesco Salviati had been working since 1539. Aretino said, 'Although the figures he is arranging appear only on the surface, the brush stroke of this admirable man follows a completely new path to find the parts which cannot be seen in the image of you which he is painting... '

A little farther in the same letter Aretino makes reference to 'many of the infinite number of soldiers', and adds, 'of the air and clouds... I do not speak'. With this painting, Titian moved at one and the same time completely away from the composition by planes receding farther and farther into the background (which was typical of the works of the fourth decade of the century) and discovered the two-dimensional plane, with the contrast between the surface, at the point where the painting becomes densely plastic, and the atmospheric void, with 'the air and clouds', which was to bring him to an all-out opposition to sculptural form and mannered gestures, and the 'swirling currents of air and light, tearing through the sky in what I might call a kind of flagellation of colour', of which Longhi wrote in 1946. The crisis Titian had undergone for so long had become resolved in the luminosity of the last period. In *The Address of Alfonso d'Avalos* this attack was already under way, and the path to be taken by Titian was indicated in the jagged flashes of light on the purple robe of the officer in the foreground, light which 'wears down' and 'consumes' – there is no better way of expressing it – the rigidity of form introduced by Salviati. With this painting there began a new period in the history of Titian's art, as can be seen by comparing *The Presentation of the Virgin in the Temple* in the Accademia, Venice, with *Ecce Homo* in Vienna (1543), or the *Urbino Venus* (1538) with any one of the versions of *Venus and the Organ-player* (painted in the 1540s), or again the portraits executed for the Urbino court with those for the Farnese family, especially the *Portrait of Ranuccio Farnese* (1542).

Because his art plumbed the depths of the accepted certainties of the Renaissance, which were expressed in the terms of a naturalistic vigour, an organic and all-embracing vision of life, Titian could not make completely his own the spirit of mannerism in the same way as Schiavone and Bassano were able to do. His familiarity with mannerist works now appears as a crisis occurring in the midst of his Renaissance view of life, a crisis of dramatic proportions that led to the attainment of an 'expressive' style. The way Titian later solved this crisis came to be a determining factor in the direction taken by younger artists, who from the beginning had been brought up in the spirit of mannerism. The disturbance caused by mannerism was shown in a new attitude to light. In the *Death of St Peter the Martyr* Vasari notes the 'flash of light in the sky which illuminates the whole countryside', so that the violent action taking place below was echoed in the violence of the blaze of light. Referring to the lost *Annunciation* of 1537, painted for the Murano cloister of Santa Maria degli Angeli and of which all that remains is the engraving by Caraglia, Aretino speaks of a 'blinding light, which comes from the rays of Paradise, from where the angels have come forth, disposed in various attitudes above the pure and shining clouds'. According to Pallucchini, 'Aretino stressed the importance of light in this work, where Titian interprets manneristically and dynamically the theme he was later to develop until the very last years of his career.'

'In the portraits painted during this period of transition, Titian relies more and more on an impressionistic treatment, brought into effect with urgent brush strokes, where form has already become of less importance than light.' (Pallucchini).

In these later portraits, the formal structures of Salviati's type of mannerism lose all ornamental qualities and are reduced to a dynamic substance which expresses the spiritual energy of the sitter. In the 1540s Titian met and frequented the greatest political figures in Europe: for the first time he portrayed the Pope, Paul III Farnese, and the Emperor Charles V in his court at Augsburg. The series of Farnese portraits, which began in Venice in 1542 with Ranuccio Farnese and was followed by the Pope, painted at Busseto, Emilia, in 1543, occupied Titian during the middle years of the decade, when he was living in Rome. This potrait of Pope Paul III gains its effectiveness from the oblique placing of the chair and figure, from the energy emanating from the hands, one resting on the arm of the chair and the other, with long, slender, but inflexible fingers, lying on the purple pocket, and from the play of light over the cape. Ortolani spoke of 'a charge of energy which completely takes hold of the bony old man, as if he were grasped in a fist ...' ('Restauro di un Tiziano', *Bollettino d'Arte*); and it seems to me that in the tense excitement of this composition, in the way the figure seizes the space of the painting, it is possible to recognize the influence of Salviati's mannerism. This method of portraying a sitter could not have been conceived at the time when Titian painted the Duchess of Urbino (*pl. 37*) only five years before. The formal and closely knit composition enhances the fantastic quality of the colour, wich is lit up by an inner light, and the dynamic and freer treatment enables the image to be constructed in a few rapid and telling brush strokes. This was the time of the portrait of Pietro Aretino (Pitti, 1545), portrayed in imposing dignity as he advances, his robe with wide lapels thown carelessly open across his chest, and in a violent tone which must have amazed those who had become too accustomed to Titian's portraiture of the fourth decade of the century. Aretino described the qualities of this portrait himself: 'Certainly it breathes, pulsates and moves the spirit in the way that I do in life.'

In his meetings with dignitaries on whom the habit of power had left its mark, or whose vital energy had become impaired by age or illness, Titian came to discover, as he progressed, the type of composition, colour and execution which best revealed the psychological and historical situation of each individual. What we know from other sources, both historical and literary, concerning the private lives of each of the great figures portrayed by Titian during these years fully confirms how penetrating his observation of them was. Historians cannot study the plots woven by Ottavio Farnese at the court of Paul III, or the victory of Charles V at the Battle of Mühlberg (1547), without some reference to the interpretations Titian gave of these figures in the *Portrait of Pope Paul III and his Grandsons,* (Naples, 1546, *pl. 44*) and *Charles V at the Battle of Mühlberg*, (Prado, 1548, *pl. 45*).

If we recall from the early period of Titian's art a world of organic forms, in which the architecture of a portrait and that of a Sacred Conversation are the same, from this later period we remember human entities: the watchful energy of Pope Paul III in the 1543 portrait, the arrogance of Aretino, the sharp and obsequious profile of Ottavio contrasting with the fury of the Pope (*pl. 44*), the sick face of Pier Luigi Farnese, Duke of Parma, enclosed in armour, the anxious eyes beside the brilliant standard (Naples, 1546), and among the group of portraits painted in Augsburg in 1548, the unforgettable one of Charles V on horseback, ' wracked by pain, tortured by gout, worn out by continuous journeys through his immense and dispersed kingdom, broken by disappointments, with rebellion and betrayal all round him, yet sitting upright on his war horse, supported by heavy armour and unbending through his inner energy ', as the French art historian Henri Hauser saw him (H. Hauser-A. Renaudet, *L'età del Rinascimento e della Riforma,* Turin 1957). Cavalcaselle has justly observed: ' that Charles was not distinguished by grandeur or majesty of shape is very evident; nor has Titian tried to falsify nature by importing flattery into the portrait. '

Between Titian's journey to Rome (1545-6) and his first journey to Augsburg (1548), most probably between October 1547 and January 1548, he painted the votive portrait of the Vendramin family (National Gallery, London *p. 23*). This was something like the Pesaro altarpiece painted twenty years earlier, with the large family kneeling on the altar steps in adoration of the Shrine of the Holy Cross, between two lighted candles in the church of St John the Evangelist. This painting combines the results of Titian's experiments after 1540 in the fields of monumental composition, in Biblical art (the *Ecce Homo* in Vienna, or the ceilings previously referred to) and the altarpiece (Venice, St John the Alms-Giver), and of portraiture (the Farnese portraits, Pietro Aretino). This work takes its place within the ambit of the great monumental concepts inspired by mannerism, which characterizes the first few years of the 1540s. The placing of the altar and of the kneeling figures, foreshortened against a sky of luminous clouds opening up behind the altar, still belongs to the period of creativity from which the ceilings for the churches of Santo Spirito and St John the Evangelist and the altarpiece for the church of St John the Alms-Giver came into being. The architectonic details and the figures are linked in a robust and dynamic composition, and emphasized by the low placing of the figures. This low placing of the base of a picture, which makes it possible to arrange the figures in space according to a plan inspired by mannerism and at the same time to project them against a sky which opens behind them, was typical of this period and a clear indication of

Men of the Vendramin Family (*see p. 40*).

the direction Titian's thought was taking. The sky, thickly covered with light clouds and glowing with an atmospheric ferment, encloses the space to form a two-dimensional plane, and 'contains' the illusionistic effect of the altar foreshortened from beneath, thus solving the problem of form by means of light, which more and more comes to represent the vehicle of the artist's spirituality, the instrument of a language meant to be 'expressive'. This solution is already apparent in the detail of the objects standing on the altar: the Cross, a precious gold jewel, framed by two lighted candles in silver candlesticks. These objects, set against a cloud-studded sky, have febrile animation, and the precious material is ablaze in a delirium for which there is no precedent in Titian's earlier work, except perhaps in the Cross on the pastoral staff of St John the Alms-Giver, although it was certainly a precedent for many later developments. The dynamic structure, intensity of colour, enhanced by the sumptuous senatorial robes, and a rapidity of execution equal to that of the portrait of Pietro Aretino, all match the daring originality of the treatment of light. This was to have even more complex developments in Venetian painting generally, especially in the work of Tintoretto, through the way it was handled in *The Martyrdom of St Lawrence* (*pl. 57*), a painting begun by Titian before 1550 and completed only ten years later. We cannot fail to notice that the Vendramin altarpiece treats the devotional theme in terms which have no precedent in Titian's art. (Compared with this work, the Pesaro altarpiece seems to be a completely Renaissance painting.) The devotional aspect must have presented him with the most compelling task, since old Gabriele Vendramin wished to commemorate the recent deaths of his brother Andrea and nephew Leonardo, in January and October 1547. They are both represented (and they alone) as enraptured by the vision of the Cross; because of this they are set apart from the worldly awareness of Gabriele and his six grandsons. Titian did not entirely succeed in avoiding the danger of a certain religious rhetoric, and I believe that if the devotional aspect of the work became such a burden and so completely entered Titian's artistic invention, this

was because the altarpiece was painted at this particular time, close to the Salviati period and immediately after Titian's journey to Rome, when he had not yet resolved the contradiction between form and light, between the integrity of form and the dissolution of space in light.
It should not be forgotten, when we seek to explain the appearance of such a work in Titian's career, that the first sitting of the Council of Trent had taken place in 1545 at the command of Paul III, and that the years 1540-50 were those when the Counter Reformation, following the intransigent line of Carafa and Ignatius Loyola, formed itself into a practical and ideological organization, the Society of Jesus. The Inquisition became particularly virulent and gained ground during the late 1540s in the towns of Italy, but it was not until the 1550s, after the advent to the papacy of Carafa as Paul IV (1555), that the destruction of heresy was to become systematic and thorough. Venice put up a firm resistance, although even here some concessions had to be made. At all events, it is clear that the context of Titian's art was, because of the position he himself had created for it by putting it at the service of the strongest, not Venetian, but European. He arrived at the court of Paul III in Rome in 1545, just about the time of the opening of the Council of Trent. He was in Augsburg in 1548, less than a year after the victory of Mühlberg. There, besides the Emperor, he painted the Elector Hans Friedrich of Saxony, who was conquered and taken prisoner at Mühlberg (the portrait is now in the Kunsthistorisches Museum, Vienna). He was present at the meetings of the Diet, with whom Charles V tried to settle the religious question on his own account, since the Diet was more malleable than the Council (the Augsburg *interim*). There can be no doubt that Titian was well aware of the events which were taking place at the time. When he went to Augsburg for the second time, in 1550-1, he must certainly have noticed, during his close attendance on the Emperor, that his religious scruples had intensified. It was on the occasion of that visit that Charles V, 'who until then had been at the height of his glory, began to show signs of wishing to

withdraw, as he later did, from wordly things, to die as a God-fearing Christian, anxious for his personal salvation' (Vasari), commissioned Titian to paint *The Holy Trinity* (Prado), known also as 'La Gloria', in which, among hordes of angels and clothed in bright raiment as on the day of the Last Judgment, are portrayed the Emperor, the Empress Isabella, their son Philip, Queen Marie of Hungary and the Infanta Juana. As has been recently shown by an examination of the iconography of this painting (C. S. Harbison, 'Counter-Reformation Iconography in Titian's "Gloria"', *The Art Bulletin*, September 1967), Titian wished to clarify any possible doubt concerning the Emperor's personal convictions, and clearly condemned the Arian heresy of the non-consubstantial nature of the Trinity. (This heresy had recurred in the works of the Spanish writer Miguel Servete (1531) and, barely a year before Titian's return to Augsburg, was virulently attacked, as being connected with Lutheran Reformation, by the Catholic writer John Cochlaeus.) The painting was delivered to Charles V in 1554 together with a *Mater Dolorosa* (Madrid, Prado, 1554), and Charles took both these paintings with him when he retired to the Monastery of St Jerome at Yuste, Estremadura, in 1556, leaving the Crown of Spain to Philip (1556) and the Imperial Crown to his brother Ferdinand (1558). Charles V was constrained by circumstances to follow a policy of prudence, having at times to disavow the conclusions reached by the Council, in order to seek a compromise between Rome and Wittenberg which could save the religious unity of his kingdom. However, he agreed in his own mind with the arguments of the orthodoxy of Rome, and during his last years suffered anguish at the thought that heretical doctrines might at some time have infected his spirit. Spain, now in the hands of his son Philip, was the country he loved above all others in his empire. Determined that the ideas of the Reformation must not be allowed to bring contamination there, he himself directed persecutions and *auto da fé* from the monastery of Yuste. In 1554 Titian also sent to Queen Marie of Hungary, the sister of Charles V, in Flanders, *Christ appearing to the Magdalen* (fragment in the Prado,

1553-4), and about the same time, executed for the church of Santa Maria di Medole, Mantua, the *Apparition of the Resurrected Christ.* He accepted Charles V's invitation to Augsburg in 1548 and so joined his fate to that of the Catholic Habsburgs. From the year 1552 he worked for Philip II and continued to do so until his death in Venice on 27 August 1576.

A theme such as *Venus with the Organ-player* (*pl. 46-7*) was born when Titian was on the threshold of these events. The naked goddess lies outstretched on a bed, playing with either a *putto* or a puppy, while a young man dressed in court costume sits at the foot of the bed, playing the organ and turning to look at Venus, as if to seek inspiration from her beauty. Beyond the wide balcony, partly closed by a curtain, there is a view at sunset, over a park (in the Madrid versions, Nos 420 and 421), and over a rural landscape (in the Berlin version). The theme is one which might have emerged in the surroundings of the European courts; the earliest treatment is probably in the painting executed for the Augsburg residence of Nicolas Perrenot Granvella, Minister to Charles V. Titian made the theme his own and, in a way no other artist of his time had done, he transferred the focal point from the alcove to the landscape, which, especially in the Granvella version (Prado, No. 421), is of a ravishing beauty, with its converging rows of trees on the horizon. Through Titian's interpretation of this subject, the episode in the alcove takes its place as part of the vitality which animates the whole cosmos. The row of trees bordering the pathway, the horizon lit by the dying rays of the sun, the blue shapes of the mountains seen here and there among the tree trunks, the lovers walking off into the distance among deer and peacocks, the shimmering light upon the marble satyr of the fountain – all nature participates in this mysterious vital force which ravishes the senses of the two lovers in the alcove and breathes in the figure of the youth and in the torpid abandon of the naked goddess. Light makes the organ reeds glow, plays over the bronze decorations of the keyboard, makes a pattern of orange on the sleeve of the organist and causes the nude figure of

Venus to palpitate with life. At this stage, Titian still experienced a sense of participation in nature for which we shall seek in vain only five years later.
In a letter dated 1554, Titian referred to his *poesie*, as he called the mythological compositions he was preparing to send to Prince Philip in Spain. He referred especially to a theme to which he later returned many times: Adonis breaking away from the embrace of Venus and dragged by wild dogs towards the fatal hunt, while Cupid dozes in the wood. The *poesia* of Venus and Adonis was repeated many times, and there are versions in the Prado and in the National Gallery, London. The London version was intended to be hung in the same room as *Danae* (Prado, completed in 1554). Titian went so far as to state in a letter to Prince Philip, 'because the Danae... was seen entirely from the front, I wanted to vary this other *poesia* and show the opposite side, so that the room in which they are to be placed may be more pleasing to the eye. I shall soon send you the *poesia* of Perseus and Andromeda which will be viewed from a different angle from these [the painting now in the Wallace Collection, London], and also Medea and Jason [if this work was ever executed, it has been lost], and I hope with the aid of God to send you, besides these, a devout work which I have had in my hands for ten years now...' (letter of 1554). This series of mythological paintings accounted for most of Titian's activity during this decade. Other works belonging to the years around 1555 include the *Venus with a Mirror* series, the best version of which is in the National Gallery of Washington (*pls 54-56*). In 1556 Titian also began for Philip II the two *poesie* of Diana: *Diana and Actaeon* (*pls 61-63*) and *Diana and Callisto* (*pls 58-60*). These were delivered in 1559 while he was engaged on two other mythological compositions: *The Rape of Europa* (Boston, Isabella Stewart Gardner Museum) and *The Punishment of Actaeon* (*pl. 68-9*). With the completion of these works we come to an end of the *poesie*, which may therefore be said to fall within the sixth decade of the century. There are no mythological compositions to be found in Titian's production for Philip II during the 1560s, even if we go through

his correspondence to extend the scope of enquiry to include works which may have been lost. Taking the production of the sixth decade of the century as a whole, one can say that portraits, as well as mythological compositions, became increasingly rare, although a few examples of portraits occurred again around 1560. Titian now became completely absorbed in the production of 'devout works'. The last group of the *poesie*, consisting of the three *Dianas* and *The Rape of Europa*, brings us to Titian's last period, which is generally considered to date from the end of the 1550s, with the Naples *Annunciation* (after 1557, *pl. 65*) and *The Crucifixion* in the Church of San Domenico, Ancona. In fact, it is obvious that there is a distance of some years between, on the one hand, *Danae* (Prado) or the group of paintings including *Venus and Adonis* (Prado) and *Perseus and Andromeda* (Wallace Collection), and, on the other hand, *The Punishment of Actaeon* (National Gallery, London) or *The Rape of Europa* (Gardner Museum, Boston). The earlier works – *Danae, Venus and Adonis, Perseus and Andromeda* – all treat the female nude in the manner which was typical of Titian's style during the first half of the 1550s with a dynamic emphasis originating in mannerism (the movement of Danae's knee in relation to the movement of the servant's arm, the action of Adonis shaking off Venus' embrace, the stylized elegance linking the movement of Andromeda, who is chained to a rock and appears suspended in a dance step at the caprice of her fluttering veil, to the descent of Perseus, suspended half-way between the sky and the open jaws of the monster). All these attitudes and movements are exactly echoed in the positions of the Old Testament patriarchs and prophets and the pagan sybil (*cf.* C. S. Harbison) in *The Holy Trinity*, painted for Charles V between 1551 and 1554. The passage quoted from Titian's letter of 1554, which accompanied these *poesie*, is illuminating: the concepts he expressed were those current among mannerist painters. He insisted on 'variety', to be 'more pleasing to the eye', and he let it be understood that this 'variety' entails 'difficulty' for the artist and is therefore a test of his skill. It is apparent that Titian had absorbed the ideas of contemporary theoreticians, Serlio, for example, who said that variety between the parts engenders great delight for the eye and satisfaction for the mind, as well as the ideas of Pino: 'Let the attitudes of the figures be varied, and gracious ... and in all your works include one figure all distorted, mysterious and difficult, so that you should become known as a talented painter by those who understand the perfection of art.' (*Biologo della Pittura*, 1548). Both these writers were popular in Venice at the time.

The question remains whether Titian's use of the term *poesie*, which Vasari employed on more than one occasion which the simple meaning of 'inventions', limited to the context of paintings with a mythological content, did not come to imply for him some special shade of meaning, in relation to the manneristic background from which they emerged and to the concepts he was developing at that stage. In any case, the meaning of the passage is clear: for Titian (at least, this is what he said) and, it would seem, for Philip also, the person who occupied the room for which these paintings were produced must be someone who could appreciate them for the qualities of their form, for the 'variety' and 'difficulty' of the artifices employed (including luministic devices), and not merely for their pagan content – in other words, the skill of the artist, not the objective narrative in these pagan myths.

In comparison with the three *poesie* painted in 1552-6, the Edinburgh *Diana and Actaeon* (*pls 61-3*) and *Diana and Callisto* (*pl. 58-9*) seem to have shed all traces of artifice and appear in an unexpectedly natural light. Among the ruins of a building overgrown by vegetation Diana and her maidens bathe under the protection of an improvised curtain. Actaeon has come upon them by chance while hunting, and his arrival is dramatically represented by the parting of the curtain, creating an area of shadow at the centre of the composition, above the pool where Diana's maidens are bathing; this places in relief the area to the right of the painting, where Diana sits in the full glare of light, her body revealed to the guilty eyes of Actaeon. The light falling on the nude body of Diana is heightened by the vicinity of the two handmaidens who are drying her, one placed in half-shadow – a prelude to Rembrandt's *Susanna and the Elders* – the other a Negress wearing a red-and-white striped robe of a richness to inspire the imagination of Veronese and the moderns. The curtain shuts off the view of the landscape through the opening of the archway. The group of bathers is placed around the pool, farther back in the midde ground of the composition, and there is a continuous flow of light and shade over the superb naked figures. The light glows with vitality, made more potent through the animation of all nature, of the sky seen through the tracery of branches and leaves, of the *bas-reliefs* on the edges of the pool, and the well in the foreground, where every flicker of light is redoubled. The focal point of the painting is the splendour of Diana's body, as if light had surged through the substance of the nude like a fire running below the skin, bringing with it a sensual animation. The dynamic element is still in evidence, as an all-pervading sense of excitement and vitality which envelops figures and landscape. This dynamic conception of light, which is manneristic in origin, no longer takes the form of the graphic elegances found in an artist like Schiavone, with 'a facile compromise between formal elegance (the influence of the school of Parma) and a ferment of colour' (Longhi, 1946). It had now developed through Titian's own experiences, based on a classical conception of life. Although he was still working on this painting and the other Edinburgh *Diana* in the summer of 1559, it is clear that by this time he was occupied only with 'details', since the paintings were ready by June of that year. It seems likely that they had been planned much earlier, in about 1556, since the same source of inspiration seems to have been behind these works and *Venus with a Mirror* (in the National Gallery, Washington), where the naked figure of Venus stands out in sumptuous beauty against the fur held back by her hand on her body (compare Diana dried by the Negro maid-servant). These two *poesie* are still typical of the paintings of the 1550s, while the two later ones, *Diana and Actaeon* and *The Rape of Europe*, begun in 1559 and continued in the following years, introduce us to the works of the seventh decade. If we could imagine a photographic sequence intended to mark this hiatus, we might insert the Naples *Annunciation* between the Edinburgh *poesie* and the London *Punishment of Actaeon*. This would not be a case of doing violence to known facts, since we know that *The Annunciation* was executed for a chapel which was consecrated in 1557, so that the painting must have been produced after that date, that is, in 1559-60, after the two Edinburgh *Dianas* and about the same time as *The Punishment of Actaeon*.

From the year 1558 Titian worked on a series of 'devout' paintings which go far beyond the point reached in the Edinburgh *poesie*: beyond the Naples *Annunciation*, the Ancona *Crucifixion* of 1558, and *The Entombment* painted for Philip II in 1559 (*pl. 66-7*). In this last painting Titian portrayed himself in the guise of St Joseph of Arimathea, and the treatment of form is still classical. The new stage in Titian's development, which was most apparent in the works of religious inspiration, had repercussions also in the conception of the *poesie*, which now became divested of the original purpose formulated in Titian's letter of 1554. The stress was now placed on their dramatic aspect.

'The heavens poured down gloom, raising troubled vapours over the earth, with a sense of Inferno and Paradise equally lost.' These words, from a well-known commentary by Longhi on the Naples *Annunciation*, might equally be applied to *The Punishment of Actaeon* (*pl. 68-9*). The clouded air is set ablaze by flashes of light, radiating from all sides in a dazzling brilliance which goes beyond the limits of form, so that form loses all consistency and even becomes unrecognizable. Fires burn among the forest trunks, where smoke slowly rises from the surface of the earth. The forest becomes one with the mass of leaden clouds brooding over the earth, with the murmuring water and glittering hedges. Sky and earth, water and forests, merge in the wild movement which carries away forms and hurtles into chaos. The apocalypse has now descended.

This interpretation of the myth in the terms of violent dramatic action leads to Titian's later works, especially *The Punishment of Marsyas*, in the Archiepiscopal Castle,

Kroměříž, and others of the same period, among them the version of *Tarquin and Lucretia* in the Fitzwilliam Museum, Cambridge (*pl. 75*), the *St Sebastian* in Leningrad, the *Ecce Homo* in St Louis, *The Crown of Thorns* in Munich (*pl. 78*), *Shepherd and Nymph* in Vienna (*pl. 76-7*) and the Prado *Self-Portrait* (*pl. 79*). These works, which were all executed after 1570, comprise a chapter in themselves. They conclude the activity of Titian which spanned almost a hundred years. This last period may be said to have three distinguishing features:

(1) Titian turned away from manneristic forms and compositions, and from a dynamic treatment (as in the case of the London *Actaeon*, where the movement the goddess is poised to make in the act of releasing the arrow is followed in the oblique trajectory of the arrow as far as Actaeon). His paintings became denuded of all artifice, sometimes balanced around the medial axis, and so bare that they tended to become archaic.

(2) 'For the former concept of harmony and beauty Titian substitutes the concept of expression: and with this new vision opens a new path to western painting.' (Pallucchini). Of the Naples *Annunciation* Longhi has said, 'Puffs of smoke rise slowly from burning incense throughout the action; they veil and unveil it, calming and ennobling its concealed paganism.' We might say the same, even more pertinently, about the Prado *Entombment*, where the pagan sources of the forms are still more apparent: the skilfully balanced figure of Christ being placed in the sepulchre decorated with *bas reliefs*, and the figure of Nicodemus, so like the Discobolus of Myron (Titian must have studied a replica of this work in the Belvedere Collections in Rome when he painted the figure of Ottavio in *Pope Paul III and his Grandsons*: see J. Shearman, *Mannerism*, 1966).

(3) Titian tended to eliminate all differences between works having a mythological source of inspiration – the *poesie* – and the 'devout works', because his paintings became so denuded of ornamentation that they became expressive to the ultimate degree, and any such distinction would therefore have acted as a limitation. On the one hand he emphasized the violent episodes in Roman history and

myth, and his interpretation of *The Rape of Lucretia* or *The Punishment of Marsyas* coincides with his interpretation of violence in the history of Christ's Passion (*The Crown of Thorns*). On the other hand, myth could no longer be revived in the Renaissance terms of the *Bacchanals* or in the manneristic terms of the *poesie*, and now became the basis of an allegory of morality.

In its final stages Titian's language took the form of a soliloquy. He himself must have been aware of this, for when we review his entire production of these last years, we see that his painting existed almost on two planes. Firstly, there were the paintings created in order to meet the demands of a patron, especially Philip II, who now desired allegorical and moralistic works. To him Titian sent in 1571 a version of *Tarquin and Lucretia* (now in the Fitzwilliam Museum, Cambridge), a much more finished work than the earlier one in the Akademie der bildenden Künste, Vienna. He followed this in 1575 with *Spain Coming to the Aid of Religion* and *Philip II Offering the Infante Don Fernando to Victory* (both in the Prado), two paintings intended to commemorate the Battle of Lepanto (1571). Then there were the works painted for Titian's own satisfaction, which met with little public success and probably remained with him in his studio. It is known that the Leningrad *St Sebastian* passed on Titian's death to the Barbarigo della Terazza family, and that *The Crown of Thorns* (Munich) remained in his studio until it was acquired by Tintoretto. While there is no doubt that these last works must have been appreciated by Venetian artists (especially Bassano, who was now an old man), it is known that they were not well liked by the public (Vasari and important dealers included). In fact they cannot be fully comprehended except through the perspective of taste opened up much later by the impressionists, especially by the last works of Monet and of Renoir, and later still, by expressionism.

Titian and the Critics

So many works of modern criticism have been devoted to Titian that it is impossible to do justice to more than a small number within the space of a short bibliography. A catalogue limited to those works which, after Cavalcaselle's monograph (J. A. Crowe-G. B. Cavalcaselle, *Titian: His Life and Times*, 2 vols, London 1877), have attempted to give a global view of Titian's art might include the following publications: G. Gronau, *Tizian*, Berlin 1900 (English ed. London 1904) and 'Tizian', *Klassiker der Kunst* (Stuttgart 1930); C. Ricketts, *Titian*, London 1910; W. Suida, *Tiziano*, Rome 1933 (with a German and French edition); H. Tietze, *Tizian, Leben und Werk*, 2 vols, Vienna 1936 (republished in an abridged version in 1950: *Titian, Painting and Drawings*, London); Th. Hetzer, *Geschichte seiner Farbe*, Frankfurt 1935 and *Tizian*, Frankfurt 1948; R. Pallucchini, *Tiziano* (lectures given in Bologna University in 1952-3 and 1953-4), 2 vols, Bologna 1953-4.
For the problem of Titian's early years, which has been and is even now the subject of special research, the following publications should be referred to, bearing in mind that the problem is the same as for Giorgione, so that here too the bibliography could be extended: O. Phillips, *The Earlier Work of Titian*, London 1897; L. Hourticq, *La jeunesse de Titien*, Paris 1919; Th. Hetzer, *Die Frühen Gemälde Tizians*, Basle 1920; A. Morassi, 'Esordi di Tiziano', *Arte Veneta*, 1954.
Fundamental studies on the last years of Titian include: the chapter by Berenson in *The Venetian Painters of the Renaissance*, New York and London 1894; the lectures given by Dvorak during a course on Italian art held in Vienna in 1918-21, and the essays of Longhi ('Giunte a Tiziano', *L'Arte*, 1925; 'Cartella tizianesca', *Vita artistica*, 1927; *Viatico per cinque secoli di pittura veneziana*, Florence 1946).
A complete bibliography with the opinions of critics on each of Titian's works and a photographic reproduction of each painting is found in F. Valcanover, *All the Paintings of Titian*, 4 vols, London, Oldbourne Press.

Flora (see p. 40).

Notes on the Plates

1 Portrait of a Man. Canvas, 50.2×45.1 cm. New York, Metropolitan Museum of Art.

2-3 Pastoral Concert. Canvas, 110×138 cm. Paris, Louvre.

4-5 Madonna and Child, St Anthony of Padua and St Roch. Canvas, 92×103 cm. Madrid, Prado.

6 Miracle of the Wounded Woman (or The Jealous Husband). Fresco, 327×183 cm. Padua, Scuola del Santo, 1511.

7 Portrait of a Woman. Canvas, 117×97 cm. London, National Gallery. On the balustrade are the initials: 'T.V.'.

8-9 Noli me tangere. Canvas, 107×97 cm. London, National Gallery.

10-11 Madonna and Child, St John the Baptist. Canvas, 90×120 cm. Edinburgh, National Gallery of Scotland. Property of Lord Ellesmere.

12-14 The Three Ages of Life. Canvas, 106×182 cm. Edinburgh, National Gallery of Scotland. Property of Lord Ellesmere. Before 1513.

15 Portrait of a Youth in a Hat. Panel, 53×42 cm. Vienna, Kunsthistorisches Museum. Unfinished.

16 Tarquin and Lucretia. Panel, 84×68 cm. Vienna, Akademie der bildenden Künste.

17 Portrait of a Girl. Panel, 64.5×51 cm. Vienna, Kunsthistorisches Museum (No. 65). Mutilated at bottom right. Once believed to be a portrait of Violante, the daughter of Palma Vecchio.

18 Salome. Canvas, 90×72 cm. Rome, Doria Gallery.

19 Woman with a Mirror. Canvas, 98×81 cm. Munich, Alte Pinakothek. Scholars believe that the mirror reflecting jewellery was added in the seventeenth century to replace a book, in order to transform the painting into an 'Allegory of Vanity'.

20-21 Madonna with St John the Baptist and a Donor. Canvas, 75×92 cm. Munich, Alte Pinakothek.

22-23 Madonna and Child, St Ulfus and St Bridget. Panel, 86×130 cm. Madrid, Prado.

24-25 Sacred and Profane Love. Canvas, 118×279 cm. Rome, Borghese Gallery. Painted for the Venetian nobleman Nicolò Aurelio (his coat of arms appears on the sarcophagus). The famous title was given in the seventeenth century and does not convey the original meaning of the invention, which is hidden in Venetian humanistic culture of the early years of the century.

26 Portrait of a Musician. Canvas, 99×82 cm. Rome, Spada Gallery. Unfinished.

27 Portrait of a Man. Canvas, 88×75 cm. Vienna, Kunsthistorisches Museum. Once thought to be the portrait of Doctor Parma, a work which has been lost.

28-29 Bacchanal. Canvas, 175×193 cm. Madrid, Prado. Signed: 'TICIANUS F'. Painted for the study of Alfonso d'Este in Ferrara (from the subject taken from the *Images* of Philostratus).

30 The Bravo. Canvas, 75×65 cm. Vienna, Kunsthistorisches Museum. Possibly identifiable with *Caius Lucius Attacking Clelius Plodius*, thought by Ridolfi to be by Giorgione.

31 Venus Anadyomene. Canvas, 73.6×58.4 cm. Edinburgh, National Gallery of Scotland. Property of Lord Ellesmere. Possibly identiable with *The Bather*, painted by Titian for Alfonso in 1517.

32 Portrait of a Man. Canvas on panel, 89×74 cm. Munich, Alte Pinakothek.

33 Portrait of a Man (Man with a Glove). Canvas, 100×89 cm. Paris, Louvre. Signed: 'TICIANUS F'.

34-35 The Entombment. Canvas, 148×225 cm. Paris, Louvre. Perhaps painted for Federigo Gonzaga, Duke of Mantua, or his mother Isabella d'Este.

36 The Magdalen. Panel, 85×68 cm. Florence, Pitti Palace. Signed: 'TITIANUS'. Painted for the Duke of Urbino.

37 Portrait of Eleonora Gonzaga, Duchess of Urbino. Canvas, 114×102.2 cm. Florence, Uffizi. 1538.

38-39 The Pardo Venus Canvas, 196×385 cm. Paris, Louvre. This painting seems to have been enlarged on the left side by the addition of a horn-player and a dog, unless this ought to be considered as part of an already existing section which has now perished. Identified as 'Nude with Landscape and Satyr', which Titian mentions in 1574 as having been sent to Philip II during the previous twenty-five years. It was formerly in the Pardo Palace in Madrid, whence its title.

40 Portrait of Francis I of France. Canvas, 109×89 cm. Paris, Louvre. Painted in 1538 from a medal by Cellini and sent as a gift by Aretino to the King of France.

41-42 The Address of Alfonso d'Avalos. Canvas, 223×165 cm. Madrid, Prado. 1540-1. D'Avalos was a marquis in the service of Charles V and fought on the Turkish front.

43 The Crown of Thorns. Panel, 303×180 cm. Paris, Louvre. Signed: 'TITIANUS F.'. Painted for the Chapel of Santa Corona in the Church of Santa Maria delle Grazie, Milan.

44 Portrait of Pope Paul III with his Grandsons. Canvas, 210×174 cm. Naples, Capodimonte Museum. Painted in Rome in 1546. Unfinished.

45 Portrait of Charles V at the Battle of Mühlberg. Canvas, 332×279 cm. Madrid, Prado. Detail with the horse's head. Painted in Augsburg, 1548.

46-47 Venus with the Organ-player. Canvas, 148×217 cm. Madrid, Prado No. 421. Signed: 'TITIANUS F.'. Probably the work painted for Nicolas Perrenot de Granvella at Augsburg in 1548.

48 Portrait of Daniele Barbaro. Canvas, 81×69 cm. Madrid, Prado.

49 Portrait of a Man with a Clock. Canvas, 122×101 cm. Once thought to be a portrait of a Knight of Malta.

50 Portrait of Antonio Anselmi. Canvas, 70×63.5 cm. Lugano, Thyssen Collection. On the reverse of the canvas is the later (but reliable) inscription: '(ANT)ONIUS ANSELMUS ANN. XXXVIII. MDL (T)ITIANUS F.'.

51 Portrait of a Man with Book and Staff. Canvas, 117×91 cm. Vienna, Kunsthistorisches Museum. Signed: 'TITIANUS F.'. Once thought to be a portrait of Benedetto Varchi.

52-53 Portrait of the Doge Francesco Venier. Canvas, 113×99 cm. Lugano, Thyssen Collection. Painted between June 1554 and June 1556.

54-56 Venus with a Mirror. Canvas, 124.5×105.5 cm. Washington, National Gallery of Art, Mellon Collection. Part of Titian's legacy to the Barbarigo family in 1581.

57 The Martyrdom of St Lawrence. Canvas, 500×280 cm. Venice, Church of the Jesuits. Commissioned by Lorenzo Massolo in 1548 for the Church of the Crociferi (now the Jesuits), and painted between 1557 and 1559.

58-60 Diana and Callisto. Canvas, 187×205 cm. Edinburgh, National Gallery of Scotland. Property of Lord Ellesmere. Signed: 'TITIANUS F.'. Painted for Philip II in 1556-9.

61-63 Diana and Actaeon. Canvas, 190.5×207 cm. Edinburgh, National Gallery of Scotland. Property of Lord Ellesmere. Signed: 'TITIANUS F.'. For Philip II in 1556-9.

64 Portrait of Fabrizio Salvaresio. Canvas, 112×88 cm. Vienna, Kunsthistorisches Museum. 'MDLVIII. FABRICIUS SALVARESIUS ANNV AGENS L. TITIANI OPUS'.

65 Annunciation. Canvas, 232×190 cm. Naples, Church of San Domenico Maggiore. Signed: 'TITIANUS FECIT'. The chapel is thought to have been consecrated in 1557.

66-67 The Entombment. Canvas, 137×175 cm. Madrid, Prado, No. 440. Signed: 'TITIANUS VECELLIUS AEQUES CAES'.

Painted for Philip II in 1559. The figure of Joseph of Arimathea is a self-portrait of Titian.

68-69 The Punishment of Actaeon. Canvas, 179×189 cm. London, National Gallery, Lord Harewood Collection. This is probably the version to which Titian referred in his letter of 1559 to Philip II.

70 St Jerome. Canvas, 184×170 cm. Escorial, New Museums (formerly in the Monastery of St Lawrence). Signed: 'TITIANUS F.'. Painted for Philip II. It is probably the painting sent to Philip in 1575, but was executed at the same time as the London *Punishment of Actaeon.*

71 Crucifixion. Canvas, 216×111 cm. Escorial. Not mentioned in the correspondence between Titian and Philip II.

72 St Jerome. Canvas, 137.5×97 cm. Lugano, Thyssen Collection.

73 Annunciation. Canvas, 410×240 cm. Venice, Church of San Salvatore. Signed: 'TITIANUS FECIT'. Before 1566, in which year Vasari saw it.

74 Portrait of Jacopo Strada. Canvas, 125×95 cm. Vienna, Kunsthistorisches Museum. Signed: 'TITIANUS F.' 1567-8. The shield with an inscription, giving the identification of the subject and the (erroneous) date 1566, goes back to the early years of the 17th century.

75 Tarquin and Lucretia. Canvas, 189×145.4 cm. Cambridge, Fitzwilliam Museum. Signed: 'TITIANUS F.'. Sent to Philip II in 1571.

76-77 Shepherd and Nymph. Canvas, 149.6×187 cm. Vienna, Kunsthistorisches Museum.

78 The Crown of Thorns. Canvas, 280×182 cm. Munich, Alte Pinakothek. In all probability this painting was among those inherited by Tintoretto from Titian.

79 Self-portrait. Canvas, 86×65 cm. Madrid, Prado.

Portrait of a Man (Man in Blue). Canvas, 81×66 cm. National Gallery, London. (*See. p. 5*).

Men of the Vendramin Family before a Relic of the True Cross. Canvas, 206×301 cm. National Gallery, London. (*See p. 23*).

Flora. Canvas, 79×63 cm. Uffizi, Florence. (*See p. 36*).

1

418.

5

7 →

6

9–

8

13

15

14

16

17

25

27

26

30

31

37

36

41–

40

43

42

45

44

53.

49

48

50

51

57-

56

← 58

59

60

61

62

63

64

65

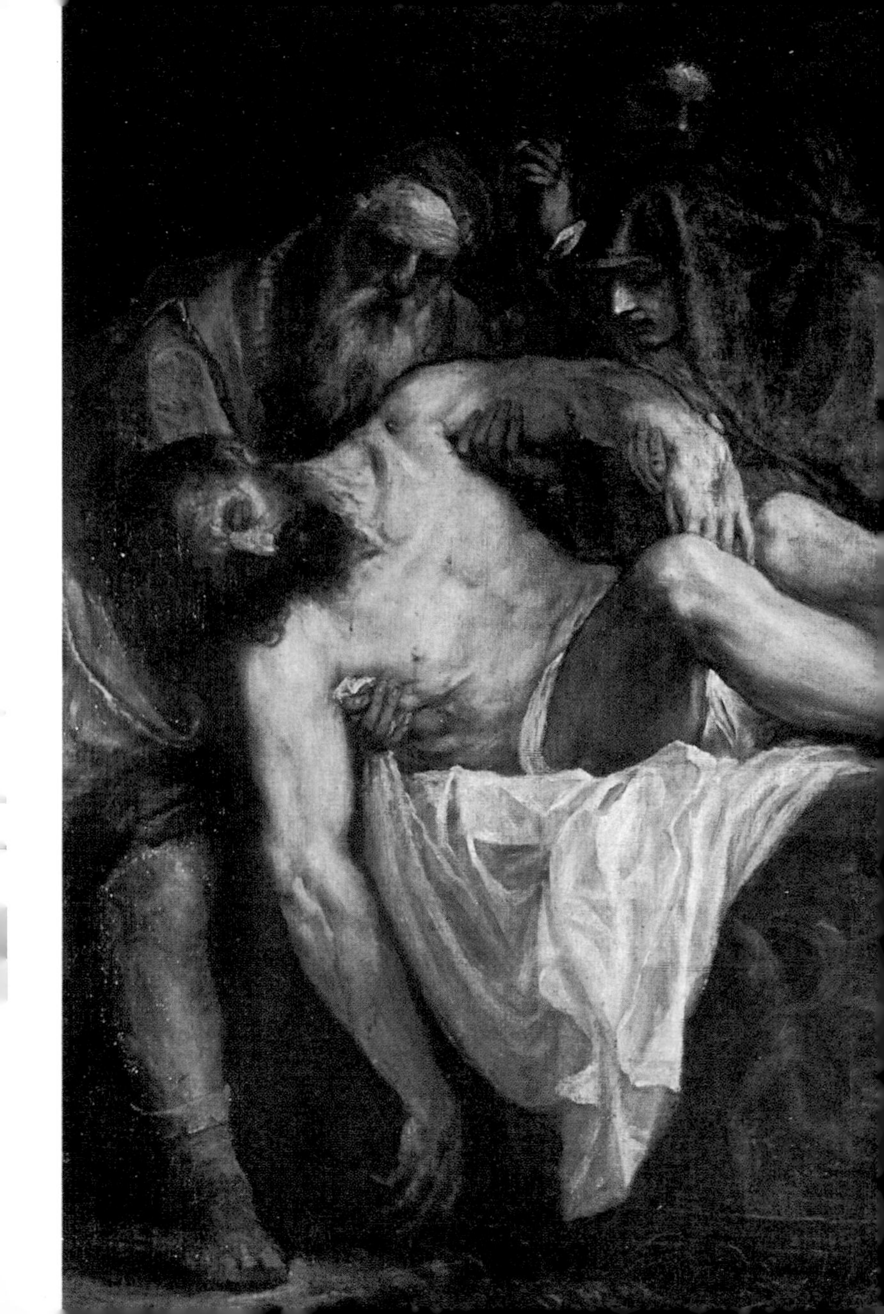

←70

71

- 72

73

ACOBVS DE
CIVIS ROMANV
NTIQVARIVS

-74

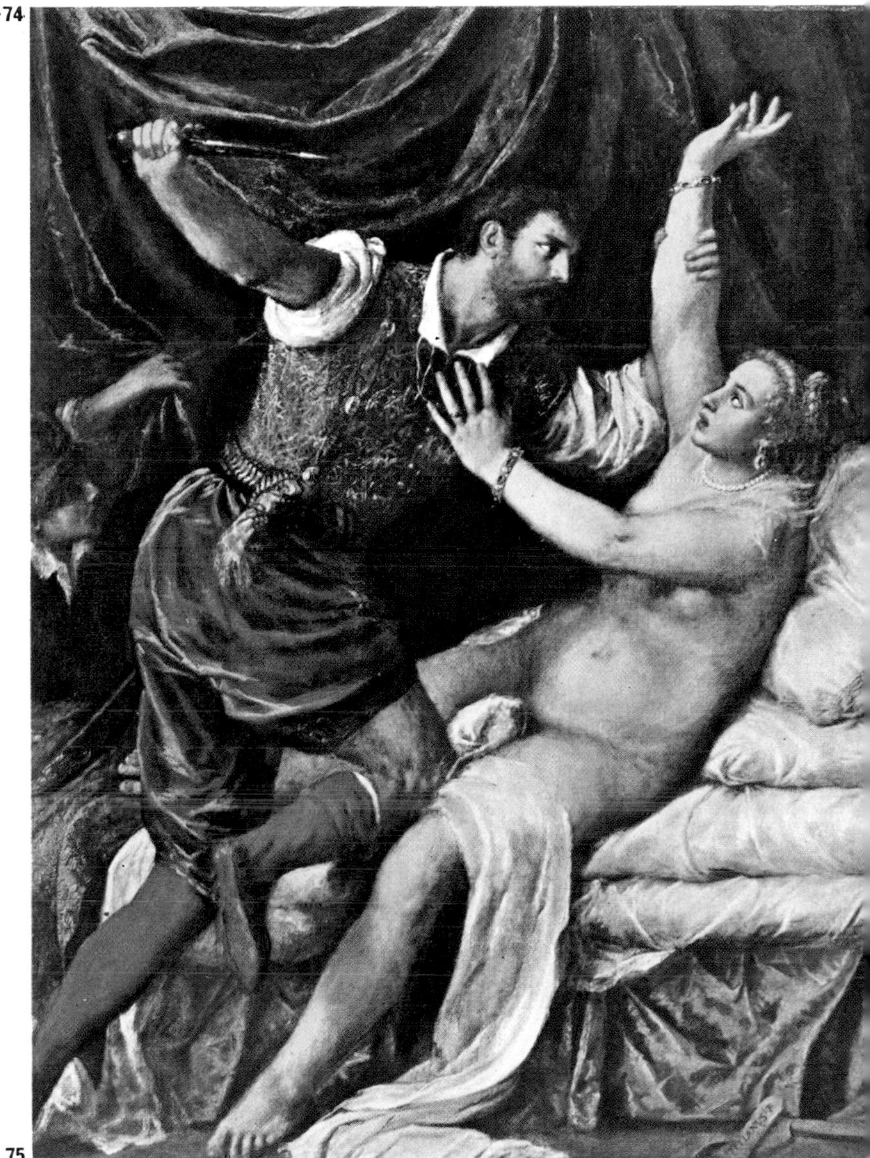

75

79